Poetry for Students, Volume 27

Project Editor: Ira Mark Milne

Editorial: Jennifer Greve

Rights Acquisition and Management: Beth Beaufore, Aja Perales, Kelly Quin, Robyn Young **Manufacturing**: Drew Kalasky

Imaging and Multimedia: Lezlie Light **Product Design**: Pamela A. E. Galbreath, Jennifer Wahi **Vendor Administration**: Civie Green **Product Manager**: Meggin Condino

For more information, contact
Gale
27500 Drake Rd.
Farmington Hills, MI 48331-3535
Or you can visit our Internet site at

attention of the publisher and verified to the satisfaction of the publisher will be corrected in future editions.

EDITORIAL DATA PRIVACY POLICY

Does this publication contain information about you as an individual? If so, for more information about our editorial data privacy policies, please see our Privacy Statement at www.gale.com.

ISBN-13: 978-0-7876-8717-5
ISBN-10: 0-7876-8717-0
eISBN-13: 978-1-4144-2935-9
eISBN-10: 1-4144-2935-5
ISSN 1094-7019

Printed in the United States of America
10 9 8 7 6 5 4 3 2 1

Goblin Market

Christina Rossetti

1862

Introduction

The English Victorian poet Christina Rossetti's allegorical poem "Goblin Market" initially appeared in *Goblin Market and Other Poems* (1862), the first volume of her poetry to be commercially published. The poem is also available in *The Complete Poems of Christina Rossetti* (1979) and the 2001 issue of the same edition, simply titled *The Complete Poems*.

"Goblin Market" is the most discussed of Rossetti's poems and is widely considered to be her greatest work. Though Rossetti always maintained that "Goblin Market" is a children's poem, the strongly erotic elements underlying what is superficially a moral lesson make it a multi-layered and complex work. It can be read as a study of female sexuality, an allegory (or symbolic story) about divine and earthly love, a celebration of female heroism, or as a metaphor for Christ's sacrifice on the cross, among many other possibilities. Most of the potential interpretations are not mutually exclusive.

"Goblin Market" and the collection in which it was first published led to Rossetti's standing as a writer of allegorical and lyric poetry. With the rise of feminist criticism in the 1980s, the poem's standing grew in tandem with an awareness of Rossetti as a notable female poet. As of the early twenty-first century, Rossetti's appeal has expanded and she is widely considered one of the greatest Victorian poets of any gender.

Author Biography

Christina Georgina Rossetti was born on December 5, 1830, in London, England, the fourth child of an Italian immigrant family with strong literary and artistic leanings. Her father, Gabrielle Rossetti, was an Italian poet and political exile whose support for revolutionary nationalism drove him to seek refuge in England. One of Rossetti's brothers was the painter and poet Dante Gabriel Rossetti. His work is also discussed and studied today. Her other brother, William Michael Rossetti, was a writer and critic who later acted as her editor. Both brothers were members of the Pre-Raphaelite Brotherhood art movement. Rossetti's sister, Maria Francesca Rossetti, was an author who later in life became an Anglican nun. Indeed, Rossetti dedicated "Goblin Market" to Maria. Rossetti's mother, Frances Polidori (later Rossetti), was the daughter of another Italian exile and the sister of John Polidori, the physician of the famous poet Lord Byron.

As a child, Rossetti was close to her maternal grandfather, Gaetano Polidori. She often stayed at his house in the Buckinghamshire countryside. She was educated at home by her mother, who periodically worked as a governess to help support the family. In the 1840s the family suffered financial difficulties due to the poor health of Rossetti's father. During this period Frances, Christina, and Maria Rossetti became deeply committed to Anglicanism (the Church of England).

Rossetti's religious faith played a major role in her life. In her late teens she became engaged to the painter James Collinson but ended the engagement when he converted to Roman Catholicism. Later she became involved with the linguist Charles Cayley but did not marry him, also for religious reasons.

The young Rossetti was of a passionate and volatile nature. Her father (cited by Mary Arseneau in the *Dictionary of Literary Biography*) called her and Dante Gabriel the "two storms" of the family. She later learned to control her temperament, and was an adult of unusual, perhaps excessive, self-restraint.

Rossetti's first book, *Verses* (1847), was published by her maternal grandfather on his own press when she was only sixteen. This collection dealt with themes that are characteristic of her later work: death, rejection by a loved one, spiritual and earthly love, the transience of love and beauty, and the importance of acceptance. Beginning in 1848, Rossetti had poems published in periodicals, sometimes using the pseudonym Ellen Alleyn. She continued to write and publish her poetry throughout her life. "Goblin Market" appeared in 1862 in *Goblin Market and Other Poems*, establishing her reputation as a major poet. Other notable editions of her work include *The Prince's Progress and Other Poems* (1866), and *Poems* (1890). She also wrote a series of poems for children that was published in 1872 as *Sing-Song: A Nursery Rhyme Book*. She published religious prose and poetry with the Society for Promoting Christian

Knowledge. In the last year of her life, she broke with the Society over its refusal to make a stand against vivisection, which she strongly opposed.

In 1853, Frances, Christina, and Gabriele moved to Frome in Somerset, England, where they attempted to run a school to improve the family finances. The school failed, and in 1854 they returned to London, where they were supported by William and Maria. During the 1860s, Rossetti did charity work at the Highgate Penitentiary, aiding fallen women (prostitutes) who wanted to change their lives. She taught them reading, writing, and sewing. Some critics and biographers believe that Rossetti's experience at the penitentiary inspired her to write "Goblin Market."

Rossetti had struggled with ill health since her teens, when a doctor (probably inadequately) diagnosed her condition as "religious mania." In 1871, she became seriously ill with Graves' disease. The illness affected her heart and permanently altered her appearance, causing her eyes to protrude. In May, 1892, Rossetti was diagnosed with breast cancer. A mastectomy performed in her home proved ineffectual, and she died in London two years later on December 29, 1894. Her brother William continued to edit and publish her poetry after her death.

Poem Summary

Lines 1-31

"Goblin Market" opens with a description of how every morning and evening, "maids," that is, unmarried and virgin women, hear goblin men advertising the fruits they have grown, with the cry, "Come buy, come buy." The goblins call out a long list of the many sorts of fruits they have brought to market, emphasizing their delicious taste and freshness, and inviting the passers-by to try them.

Lines 32-63

This section introduces the "maids" mentioned in the previous lines. They are two sisters, Laura and Lizzie. As they lie beside a stream in a loving embrace, Laura listens intently to the goblin men's cries while Lizzie blushes with embarrassment. Laura cautions Lizzie that they must not look at the goblin men or buy their fruits, as the fruits are grown in unfamiliar and unknown soil. In spite of her own words, Laura is apparently unable to resist taking a peep at the goblin men, as Lizzie, covering her own eyes, rebukes Laura for looking at them. Laura sees the goblin men walking into the valley bearing baskets of fruit and thinks that the vines and bushes that bear such crops must be exceptionally beautiful.

Lines 64-80

Lizzie sternly warns Laura that they should not be charmed by the goblins' fruit, which would harm them if they were to taste it. Lizzie puts her fingers in her ears, shuts her eyes, and runs away from the goblin market. But Laura, overcome with curiosity, lingers to watch the goblins. They have animal characteristics: one has a cat's face, another a tail, and so on. Their voices are described as kind and loving, like doves cooing.

Lines 81-104

Laura's self-restraint breaks down. She attempts to get a closer look at the goblin men. Seeing her curiosity, they carry their baskets of fruit back along the valley to where Laura is standing. They put their baskets down and offer her dishes of fruit. One begins to weave a crown for her of leaves, tendrils, and nuts. They continue their cry, "Come buy, come buy."

Lines 105-140

Laura gazes longingly at the fruit. A goblin with a tail suggests that she taste it. The goblins speak smoothly and welcomingly to her. Laura says that she has no money, so if she were to take their fruit, she would be stealing. She says that the only gold she has is the yellow flowers of the bushes that grow on the heath. In unison, the goblin men reply that she has gold on her head, meaning her blonde hair, and they will accept a lock of hair as payment for their fruit. Laura sheds a tear and hungrily sucks at the fruits' juices. She sucks until her lips are sore and throws the rinds away. She picks up a stone (pit) from one of the fruits she has eaten and returns home in such a state of intoxication that she does not know if it is night or day.

Lines 141-162

Lizzie meets Laura at the gate and rebukes her for staying out so late. Twilight, she says, and loitering in places frequented by goblin men, "is not good for maidens." Lizzie reminds Laura of a girl named Jeanie, who met the goblin men in the moonlight, ate their fruit, and wore their flower garlands. Afterwards, Jeanie unsuccessfully looked for the goblins at every opportunity, trying to purchase more fruit. Jeanie ultimately pined away and died. No grass will grow on her grave, and the daisies that Lizzie has planted there do not flower.

Lines 163-198

Laura tries to calm her sister. She says that she wants more fruit and will attempt to find the goblin men again tomorrow night. She describes the wonderful fruits she has eaten, and offers to bring Lizzie some tomorrow.

Lines 199-252

The next day, the sisters rise at dawn. They

gather honey from their beehives, milk the cows, bake cakes, make butter and cream, and feed the poultry. Then they sit and sew, and talk together. Lizzie is her usual contented self, but Laura seems distant and somewhat sick. Laura longs for nightfall.

Twilight comes, and the sisters go to the stream to collect water. As soon as they're done, Lizzie tries to bring her sister home with her, but Laura complains that the riverbank is steep and loiters there. Laura intently listens for the goblins' cry of "Come buy, come buy," but she cannot hear or see a single goblin. Lizzie, on the other hand, can hear and see the goblins. She refuses to look in their direction and begs Laura to come home with her before it gets too dark, when they could become lost.

Lines 253-298

Laura becomes cold when she realizes that her sister can hear and see the goblins and that she herself cannot. She trudges home with her sister in silence, the water dripping from her jug. After Lizzie is asleep, Laura sits in bed and weeps bitterly.

As the days pass, Laura keeps looking for the goblin men, but she never sees them or hears them. Her hair turns gray and she becomes weaker. One day, she remembers the fruit stone that she kept. She puts it next to a south-facing wall and waters it with her tears, hoping that it will sprout, but it does not. Desperate for another taste of the goblins' fruit, she dreams of it, which only increases her hunger. She neglects her domestic duties, becomes listless, and will not eat.

Lines 299-328

Lizzie is upset by her sister's suffering. As she hears the goblins' call every night and morning, she longs to buy fruit to comfort her sister, but fears the consequences in light of Jeanie's fate. Jeanie should have married but instead fell sick and died "for joys brides hope to have." The "joys" refer to the goblins' fruit. Thus, the fruit is presented as acceptable for married women, but not for unmarried ones.

When Laura is almost dying, Lizzie decides that she must act. She puts a silver penny in her purse and goes to the goblin market. For the first time in her life, she actively seeks the goblins.

Lines 329-407

The goblins greet Lizzie warmly with hugs and kisses, making strange faces and grimacing. They offer their fruits to her, inviting her to taste them. Lizzie, remembering Jeanie, is careful not to do so. Instead she throws them her silver penny, and asks to buy a large number of fruits. They refuse to take the penny, asking her to sit and eat with them as their honored guest. Lizzie refuses politely, saying that she must go home. If they will not sell her any fruit, she says, she would like her penny back.

The goblins grow angry and accuse Lizzie of being too proud and ill-mannered to sit with them. They begin to attack her physically, stamping on her feet, pulling out her hair, and tearing her dress. They try to force their fruits into her mouth.

Lines 408-474

As the goblins try to kick, pinch, and cajole Lizzie into submission, she simply stands still in silence and does not respond to the attack. She refuses to open her mouth and allow them to force in the fruit, but in the struggle, the fruits' juices are smeared all over her face and neck. At last, the goblins give up, worn out by Lizzie's resistance. They throw her silver penny back at her and retreat, kicking their fruit along the path before them. Lizzie runs home, laughing inwardly.

As Lizzie approaches her house, she shouts for Laura to come out and kiss her. In her passionate cry, "Eat me, drink me, love me," Lizzie asks her sister to suck the goblin fruit juices from her face. She explains that she has braved evil for Laura's sake.

Lines 475-542

Laura reacts to Lizzie's news with horror because she believes that Lizzie has eaten the goblin fruit. Laura fears that her sister's life will be ruined just as her own has been. But, unable to resist a taste of the goblin fruit, Laura kisses Lizzie hungrily. The juices begin to burn her mouth, and she goes into a mania, leaping, singing, and tearing her dress until she faints.

Lizzie sits awake by her sister's side all night long. The next morning, Laura awakes, laughs in her old innocent way, and hugs Lizzie. Her unhealthy desire for the goblin fruit has disappeared.

Lines 543-567

The last lines of the poem function as an epilogue, or a concluding section that rounds out the narrative. The poem jumps ahead in time by many years, when both sisters are married and have children. Laura tells her children the story of her encounter with the goblin men, of how their fruit poisoned her, and of how her sister risked her own life to save her. Laura joins the hands of her children together as she teaches them the moral of the story: that in order to stay virtuous "there is no friend like a sister."

Earthly and Divine Love

"Goblin Market" draws a contrast between earthly and divine love. Earthly love (physical or sexual) can be a distraction from divine (spiritual or nonphysical) love. Earthly love, embodied by Laura, is portrayed as selfish. Divine love, in contrast, embodied by Lizzie, is selfless and self-sacrificial. Motivated by a selfless (divine) love for her sister, Lizzie sacrifices herself by exposing herself to the goblins' temptations and their ensuing attack. She withstands both, maintaining her virtue. This selfless act is rewarded, as Lizzie is now able to save her sister's life with the fruit juices smeared upon her face.

As an application of this theme, it is possible to interpret the two sisters as aspects of the same psyche: the selfish, materialistic side (Laura), and the selfless, spiritual side (Lizzie). Winston Weathers presents this interpretation in his essay "Christina Rossetti: The Sisterhood of Self." As all humans have these aspects, the combined sisters thus become a kind of everywoman. In this interpretation, the poem becomes a story of conflict within the psyche between the materialistic and spiritual aspects of humankind, and the epilogue showing the two sisters as married with children represents the psyche's return to unity. This interpretation is visually supported by the indistinguishable appearance of the two sisters (both are golden-haired beauties), and by their habit of sleeping and resting in a close embrace.

Female Sexuality

Many critics point to the homoerotic tone of the poem, commenting that Laura and Lizzie are more like lovers than sisters. They lie in close embrace, "With clasping arms and cautioning lips, / With tingling cheeks and finger tips." The poem abounds with torrid lines such as "She kissed and kissed her with a hungry mouth." Yet the love between the sisters is portrayed as pure and divine. The heterosexual relationships, in contrast, between the sisters and the male goblins, are portrayed as an evil seduction (when Laura eats the goblins' fruit) and as an attempted rape (when the goblins try to force Lizzie to eat their fruit). The homoerotic theme is underlined by the lack of a male hero and by Lizzie's assumption of this classical role.

Topics for Further Study

- Rossetti's "Goblin Market" has been illustrated by (among others) three famous artists: Dante Gabriel Rossetti, Laurence Housman, and Arthur Rackham. Study some of these illustrations. (They are available on the Internet and also in older print editions of the poem.) Write an essay explaining what each illustration contributes to your understanding of the poem. Note the incidents or characters that the artists choose to illustrate and how their choices shift the emphasis to different aspects of the poem. Note whether each illustration reflects or enhances the dramatic power of Rossetti's narrative, and why.

- Create your own set of at least three illustrations of "Goblin Market" and give a class presentation on what you were trying to convey about the poem in your work.

- Research the Pre-Raphaelite artistic movement. Based on your findings, write an essay explaining any Pre-Raphaelite influence you detect in "Goblin Market." Include a section on the ways in which you feel Rossetti departs from the conventions of the Pre-Raphaelite movement in her poem.

- Research the role of women in Victorian England with relation to either sexual attitudes and politics, art and literature, or commerce. Identify women who were pioneers, activists, writers, or thinkers in these fields. What was their view of women's role or status? How did they want to change things? Did anything finally change, and if so, why and how? Create a video on your findings and present your video to the class.

- Write a poem in which you describe a temptation that you have faced, and in which you express the outcome of your giving in to, or resisting, that temptation.

Female Heroism and Solidarity

Though female protagonists were common in literature in and before the Victorian age, female heroes (people distinguished by extraordinary courage or ability) were extremely rare. Convention demanded that any heroic action in defense of purity, such as the act that Lizzie performs in the poem, was made by men. Lizzie is therefore unusual in her single-handed rescue of her fallen sister. It is true that her heroic action is of a passive nature: she does not fight the goblins, but merely stands still and keeps her mouth firmly shut against the fruit until they give up. But it could be argued that passive resistance, as in Mahatma Gandhi's campaign to drive the British occupiers out of India, can be effective. It is also, crucially, the tactic that Christ used when dealing with his persecutors. His death on the cross was marked by passive suffering. As Lizzie shares some Christ-like qualities, her passive demeanor fits Rossetti's purpose.

Lizzie's saving of Laura gives rise to the last lines of the poem in praise of sisters as the best possible supporters and friends. While these lines are so trite and moralistic that they appear to be from a different poem altogether, the poem's predominantly sensual and passionate treatment of the deep bond between the sisters clearly shows Rossetti's promotion of female heroism and solidarity.

Societal Anxieties and the Supernatural

The Victorians were extremely interested in fairies and the land in which they were supposed to live, which was termed *Faerie*. Fairies both frightened and fascinated Victorians in equal measure, becoming a repository of many qualities and activities that were considered alien or threatening to respectable society. These included sexual power and appetite (particularly of the female variety), physical deformity, human difference or strangeness, and everything deemed irrational and unscientific. Some of these anxieties are evident in "Goblin Market." The goblins are male, and they tempt maidens with their illicit fruit. In essence, they are agents of male sexual passion, and the appetite they awaken in Laura for their fruit is clearly symbolic of feminine sexual desire. The goblins' sexual nature is underlined by their animal characteristics, as animals were often used to symbolize base appetites. Base appetites, such as sexual desire, were viewed by Victorians as the cause of most sin. This is also why the devil is often portrayed as being half animal and half human in form.

Furthermore, it was traditionally believed that silver offered protection against the mischief of fairies. This is why Lizzie insists on paying for the goblins' fruit with a silver penny.

Style

Allegory

An allegory is a representation of an abstract or spiritual meaning through concrete or material forms. Although Rossetti reportedly denied that "Goblin Market" had any deeper meanings, it seems clear that, whatever her conscious intention, deeper meanings are indeed present. Certainly, critics have always dismissed her claim, and have discussed the poem as an allegory of a variety of possible themes. These include temptation, the biblical Fall of Adam and Eve, and redemption; the contrast between earthly and divine love; the triumph of selfless love over selfish lust; the importance of female solidarity in a world dominated by hostile males; and the superiority of society over the individual. Some critics propose that the poem represents the affirmation of the domestic role for women in preference to activity in the masculine world of commerce (as represented by the consequences of going to the goblin market), while others suggest that the poem represents female heroism in a male-dominated world. But in fact, none of these interpretations excludes another. Rosetti's poem has remained under discussion for over 100 years for this very reason; it is successful because it is an open-ended allegory with many feasible, nonexclusive symbolic meanings.

Symbolism

The major symbol of the poem is the goblin fruit. The fact that eating the goblin fruit or even looking at the goblin men is out-of-bounds for "maids" suggests that it is symbolic of illicit sexual passion that tempts women away from chastity and virtue. This is underlined by Rossetti's portrayal of the fruit as juicy, and full of apparent vitality. The image of Laura sucking hungrily on the fruit "until her lips were sore" is loaded with sexuality.

As an extension of this symbolism, the goblin fruit can be seen as representing the biblical forbidden fruit that tempts Eve into sin. It is noteworthy that after Adam and Eve taste the forbidden fruit, for the first time they feel sexual shame and cover their genitals with fig leaves. After this so-called Fall, they lose their innocence (they are ejected from the Garden of Eden) and their lives are filled with suffering. This turn of events is similar to Laura's experiences after she has eaten the goblins' fruit.

Laura's suffering is such that she can never fully satisfy her hunger for more goblin fruit. This is emblematic of the inability of mankind (all of whom are fallen as they are the descendants of Adam and Eve) to gain true happiness from the pleasures of the material world. The poem shows that these pleasures only serve as distractions from the true and fulfilling love of God (symbolized by Lizzie's contentment, and her subsequent self-sacrifice for her sister).

Jeanie is not saved by the intervention of a loving sister, and though she "should have been a bride," she can never marry because she has been defiled. The implication is that the defilement is sexual, as previously unmarried women in Victorian society were considered unmarriageable if they were not virgins, even if they had been raped. Thus, the only way forward for Jeanie is death because societal views at the time considered a defiled woman useless and subsequently better off dead (this belief is still held by some cultures today). Rossetti here reflects the strong expectation of her time that women should be virgins when they married and that the only place for sexuality was within marriage. Sexual passion outside marriage was viewed as sinful, but the sacrament of marriage was a way of legitimizing such passion as a tool solely for the purpose of procreation. The last lines of the poem, which show the previously fallen Laura as a happily married woman teaching her children moral lessons about the value of a sister, support this interpretation.

Rhyme Scheme and Meter

The poem uses an irregular rhyme scheme. There are many couplets (where two consecutive lines rhyme with each other) resulting in *aabb* rhyme patterns. Sometimes rhymes are repeated over three consecutive lines. At other points, several lines go by before a rhyme is completed. Internal rhymes, where the syllable that completes a rhyme appears in the middle rather than at the end of the line, are also used, as in "Her hair grew thin and gray; *She dwindled, as the fair full moon doth turn* To swift decay and burn / Her fire away," where the rhymes fall on the words *gray*, *decay* (the internal rhyme), and *away*. In addition, the ending syllables of the last two lines rhyme with their ending words *turn* and *burn*.

The meter is irregular, though generally there are four or five stresses in each line.

Recurring Imagery

Images of fire are used to describe Laura's hunger for the goblin fruit. During the sisters' walk to the stream, shortly after Laura has eaten the fruit, she is described as being "like a leaping flame" in her eager anticipation of meeting the goblins again. During her illness, she is compared to a waning moon that "doth turn / To swift decay and burn / Her fire away." The fire imagery is used to emphasize the destructive nature of Laura's actions and also connotes the flames of hell.

Imagery of night and day, or darkness and light, is used to symbolically illustrate the events of the poem. The goblins, as sinister creatures of darkness, appear during the evening twilight. Lizzie warns her sister, "Twilight is not good for maidens." After Laura's first taste of the goblin fruit, she "knew not was it night or day," which symbolically points to her loss of moral sensibility. The line indicates that Laura can no longer recognize right from wrong. Before Laura's illness takes hold, she gets up at dawn with her sister to perform her duties. But already, she is "longing for the night." As expected, Laura loiters by the stream in the evening, attempting to obtain fruit from the goblins, ignoring her sister's plea to return home "before the night grows dark." Now, darkness is Laura's element, and she seems to grow more and more ill as "the noon waxed bright." After Laura is redeemed by her sister, in contrast, the darkness retreats and the "light danced in her eyes."

Images of life and death also recur, often with relation to natural phenomena and seasons, and they convey spiritual qualities. The fruit's glowing vitality is an illusion. It has deathly qualities, as surrounding imagery tells the reader: it is offered in the twilight, and it is unnatural, as it is grown in a place "Where summer ripens at all hours." When Laura tries to sprout the fruit pit that she saves from her feast, it will not grow because "It never saw the sun." Lizzie, seeing Laura's decline, thinks of Jeanie, whose grave is barren, as the flowers planted on her grave refuse to bloom. Jeanie died at the first snowfall of winter, traditionally viewed as a season of death. Laura's return to health is marked by the birds and plants coming back to life at the onset of spring, traditionally viewed as a season of birth. Indeed, her breath is described as being as "sweet as May." The life-affirming imagery reaches its peak in the final picture of Laura with her children.

The Pre-Raphaelite Brotherhood

Both of Rossetti's brothers, Dante Gabriel and William Michael, were members of the Pre-Raphaelite Brotherhood art movement, founded in 1848. The Pre-Raphaelites focused on the detailed study of nature and their subject matter was drawn from morally uplifting stories and legends, often from the Bible, or from medieval tales of honor and chivalry. The movement was strongly Christian. The Pre-Raphaelite movement was a rebellion against Victorian materialism and artistic neoclassicism, a movement that promoted order and symmetry. Members believed that the Italian artist Raphael (1483-1520) was responsible for introducing a mechanic tendency into art, and hence they adopted the name *Pre-Raphaelite*. They looked to the Italian and Flemish art of the 1400s for their models, emulating the intense colors, complex compositions, and fine detail.

Compare & Contrast

- **1860s:** Women in the United Kingdom are not allowed to vote; in fact, the 1832 Reform Act specifically disenfranchised women.

  Today: Women in the United

Kingdom may vote and there are many female members of Parliament. From 1979 to 1990, the country had its first female prime minister, Margaret Thatcher.

- **1860s:** The Contagious Diseases Acts are passed by the United Kingdom Parliament in 1864, 1866, and 1869. The Acts allow plain-clothed police to examine prostitutes for signs of venereal disease and require them to undergo mandatory medical examination and treatment in locked hospitals. The prostitute's male clients are not affected by the Act.

  Today: In the United Kingdom, sexually transmitted diseases are treated under the government-subsidized National Health Service in specialized clinics. Attendance is voluntary and the clinics trace all the sexual partners (male and female) of infected individuals in order to offer them treatment. The confidentiality of infected people is preserved.

- **1860s:** Female sexuality is seldom openly discussed or expressed in art, literature, or society in general. Artistic and literary expressions of female sexuality are often symbolically coded or appear to emerge against the artist's conscious intention.

Today: Female sexuality is openly discussed in a wide variety of media. Many bookshops and adult stores have sections devoted to female-oriented erotica.

- **1860s:** Belief in fairies is widespread across a broad section of society, and fairies abound in the literature and visual art of the period. Psychologists observe that they act as a repository for a number of social anxieties prevalent in Victorian England, such as female sexual power, physical deformity, and class and racial difference.

Today: Belief in fairies has largely been replaced by belief in extraterrestrial beings, or aliens. Psychologists observe that they act as a repository for a number of social anxieties prevalent in contemporary Western society, such as the dehumanizing effects of modern science, the invasiveness of modern medical procedures, and the destructive potential of certain technologies such as nuclear missiles.

Although Rossetti herself sometimes modeled for Pre-Raphaelite artists, she was never officially a member of the movement. However, many critics, including Dorothy Mermin ("Heroic Sisterhood in 'Goblin Market'"), see Pre-Raphaelite influences in Rossetti's poetry in general and in "Goblin Market" in particular. Mermin suggests that Rossetti uses elements of the Pre-Raphaelite artistic movement in the poem, particularly the visual images, the heroic theme, and "the erotic and imaginative intensity" that the movement favored. But, according to Mermin, she subtracts them from the overwhelmingly male viewpoint expressed in the Pre-Raphaelite works.

Female Sexuality in Victorian England

Victorian England has become a byword for sexual repression, particularly in relation to women. Women were expected to be virgins when they married for the first time, though the same standard was not applied to men; doctors removed women's sexual and reproductive organs because they were thought to be a cause of mental illness (the words *hysterical* and *hysteria* are derived from the Greek word for the uterus); and respectable women were not supposed to enjoy sex or to seek it.

Hypocrisy abounded, as can be seen from the social problems of the time. Prostitution was common, and the children that were idealized as innocence personified were sent to hard labor in factories and sent as sweeps up chimneys.

On the other hand, many progressive ideas and movements emerged in Victorian times, and modern historians see it as an age of contradictions rather than solid repression. Some doctors and psychologists of the day actually promoted sexual expression for women, and the social and political reform organizations acting, for example, on behalf of prostitutes or working women, proliferated. Notably, the stereotypical image of Queen Victoria and her husband Prince Albert as sexually naive and repressed has been shown by biographers to be inaccurate. The Queen of England was simply careful about her public image because she knew that loose morals among the monarchy and aristocracy had historically led to public hostility towards those institutions.

In matters of both sexual repression and sexual license, women were held to a double standard. While sexually active women were seen as guilty and in need of punishment, men were not condemned or punished for sexual license. Indeed, men may have even been encouraged to make sexual conquests.

An example of these double standards was a set of laws called the Contagious Diseases Acts, the first of which was passed in the United Kingdom in 1864. These laws forced prostitutes to undergo inspections for venereal diseases. If signs of the disease were found, the woman could be locked up in a prison hospital for up to three months, where she was subjected to the brutal treatments of the time. Though it was claimed that the purpose of the law was to prevent the spread of venereal disease, the male clients of the prostitutes were never inspected. It was assumed that inspecting men was an unacceptable intrusion into privacy, whereas the women were so far degraded that further humiliation was of no consequence.

At first glance, "Goblin Market" seems to conform to conventional notions of female sexual transgression, and Laura's wasting sickness after eating the goblin fruit my be seen as a deserved punishment. Her illness also undoubtedly reflects contemporary concerns about venereal diseases such as syphilis. But Rossetti subverts contemporary attitudes about fallen women in her redemption of Laura, who, unusually in literature, goes on to marry happily and have children.

Women and Economic Power in Victorian England

Married women in Western societies were not allowed to personally own property until the late nineteenth century. If a property-owning woman married, her property automatically became her husband's. Most single women also had no money of their own, going immediately from their father's care to their husband's when they married. Laura, in common with many women in Victorian England, has no money of her own ("I have no coin," she says) so she must pay for the fruit with part of herself, a lock of hair. This may be a comment on the commodification of women in the marriage market, in that the only commodity that women could use to bargain with was their bodies, as that was the only thing they truly owned. Lizzie is careful to take a silver penny with her when she goes to the goblin market, insisting on paying with money rather than giving the goblins a piece of herself. The goblins' fury at this can be interpreted as male resistance to Victorian women's attempts to gain economic freedom and equality.

The Industrial Revolution and Society

The Industrial Revolution began in England in the late eighteenth century and reached its peak in the mid-nineteenth century, around the time that Rossetti wrote "Goblin Market." Writers such as the poet William Blake (1757-1827), the novelist Elizabeth Gaskell (1810-65), and the critic (and friend of the Rossettis) John Ruskin (1819-1900) wrote at length about the social problems and anxieties caused by the Industrial Revolution. In particular, there was concern that relationships and interactions previously based on human values were becoming tainted by financial transactions. In parallel with these concerns, there arose a heightened appreciation and idealization of the rural activities and trades that were rapidly being abandoned as thousands flocked to the cities in order to work in factories. The rural trades, it was believed, tied man to nature and resulted in innocent and happy lives. The factories, on the other hand, were seen as hellish, filthy, unhealthy places that enslaved, degraded, and separated people from sustaining nature.

Rossetti introduces such concerns and idealizations into her poem. The goblins are men and they are merchants, so they can be seen as symbolizing agents of the almost exclusively male-controlled Industrial Revolution. The two sisters, in contrast, are engaged in purely rural activities such as milking cows, keeping bees, and making cakes. Their troubles begin when they venture into the commercial world of the goblins. The goblins' attempts to seduce Laura and Lizzie with their fruit could be seen as parallel to commercial advertising. The gain for the goblins if the women buy, however, is not money, but the women's bodies and souls. This may be a comment on the degrading nature of a society based on commerce.

Critical Overview

In 1861, Dante Gabriel Rossetti sent "Goblin Market" to the influential critic John Ruskin in the hope that he would recommend it to William Makepeace Thackeray, the editor of *Cornhill* magazine. But Ruskin (cited by Mary Arseneau in the *Dictionary of Literary Biography*) was largely unimpressed. He praised the poem's "beauty and power" but claimed that nobody would publish it because of its many "quaintnesses and offences." About the irregular meter that has been so praised by more recent critics, Ruskin commented, "Irregular measure ... is the chief calamity of modern poetry ... your sister should exercise herself in the severest commonplace of metre until she can write as the public like." Fortunately, Alexander Macmillan of the Macmillan publishing company disagreed, and the following year he brought out Rossetti's first commercially published volume of poetry, *Goblin Market and Other Poems* in 1862.

The collection was an immediate critical success and received many favorable reviews in the year of publication, including in the *London Review*, the *Spectator* and the *Saturday Review* (all cited by Mary Arseneau in the *Dictionary of Literary Biography*). A reviewer for the *Athenaeum* (April 26, 1862) describes "Goblin Market" as "suggestive and symbolical without the stiffness of set allegory." In a comment on the entire collection that could apply to "Goblin Market," the reviewer compares the experience of reading Rossetti's poems after other contemporary poetry to "passing from a picture gallery, with its well-feigned semblance of nature, to the real nature out-of-doors which greets us with the waving grass and the pleasant shock of the breeze." The reviewer notes that "Goblin Market" can be read as a simple legend, or with attention to "an inner meaning for all who can discern it."

Caroline Norton, reviewing the collection for *Macmillan's Magazine* (September 1863), remarked on the ambiguity of "Goblin Market": "Is it a fable? —or a mere fairy story—or an allegory against the pleasures of sinful love—or what is it? Let us not too rigorously inquire, but accept it in all its quaint and pleasant mystery." Norton, in common with the reviewer for the *Athenaeum*, notes that the poem can be read on different levels: on the level of a simple ballad for children, or as a work that "riper minds may ponder over."

The poem continued to attract critical interest throughout the twentieth century. In the Autumn 1956 issue of the *Victorian Newsletter*, the critic Marian Shalkhauser examines "Goblin Market" as a "Christian fairy tale") in which Lizzie symbolizes Christ and Laura represents "Adam-Eve and consequently all of sinful mankind." In his book *Wonder and Whimsy: The Fantastic World of Christina Rossetti*, Thomas Burnett Swann emphasizes the alien, imaginative, and fantastic elements of the poem. He calls "Goblin Market" "a masterpiece, because, like a child's daydream, it is both terrifying and unspeakably beautiful."

From the 1980s, the poem attracted much attention from feminist critics, among them Dorothy Mermin. Mermin argues that the cheerfulness and energy of the poem and its serene ending make it "not a poem of bitter repression but rather a fantasy of feminine freedom, heroism, and self-sufficiency and a celebration of sisterly and maternal love." As of the early twenty-first century, partly as a result of the feminist critics' work and partly because of a growing fascination with biographies of Rossetti, the poem's appeal has widened. It continues to be read and studied, and its complexities continue to be analyzed.

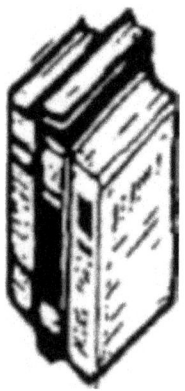

What Do I Read Next?

- "Goblin Market" ends with a tribute to sisters. Rossetti's poems "Sister Maude" and "Noble Sisters" (both first published in *Goblin Market and*

Other Poems in 1862) present very different relationships between pairs of sisters. In each poem, one sister suffers treachery at the hands of another.

- Samuel Taylor Coleridge's poem "The Rime of the Ancient Mariner" (first published in *Lyrical Ballads* in 1798), like "Goblin Market," has as its theme temptation, sin, and redemption through suffering. It shares with Rossetti's poem supernatural elements and the use of symbolism.

- *Forbidden Journeys: Fairy Tales and Fantasies by Victorian Women Writers* (1993), edited by Nina Auerbach and U. C. Knoepflmacher, is a collection of fairy tales written by women in the 1860s and 1870s. Each story's plot features a girl's journey to forbidden or strange places and thus explores unexpected emotional areas. Aside from stories by Rossetti, the book includes stories by Jean Ingelow, Anne Thackeray Ritchie,Maria Molesworth, Juliana Horatia Ewing, and Frances Burnett.

- *The Making of Victorian Sexuality* (1995), by Michael Mason, argues that Victorian attitudes toward sexuality were more progressive than are commonly thought. He neither endorses the stereotypical perception of Victorian prudery nor implies that the age was characterized by extreme sexual license. Instead, he provides evidence of evolving practices and beliefs about sexuality that in some cases seem surprisingly modern.

- In *Suffer and Be Still: Women in the Victorian Age* (1973), editor Martha Vicinus brings together a collection of essays about different aspects of the life of Victorian women. The essay topics include prostitution, working class women, economic status and power, and marriage.

Sources

Arseneau, Mary, "Christina Rossetti," in *Dictionary of Literary Biography*, Vol. 240, *Late Nineteenth- and Early Twentieth-Century British Women Poets*, edited by William B. Thesing, The Gale Group, 2001, pp. 210-31.

King James Bible, http://www.hti.umich.edu/k/kjv/ (accessed February 28, 2007).

Mermin, Dorothy, "Heroic Sisterhood in 'Goblin Market,'" in *Victorian Poetry*, Vol. 21, No. 2, Summer 1983, pp. 107-18.

Norton, Caroline, "'The Angel in the House' and 'The Goblin Market,'" in *Macmillan's Magazine*, Vol. 8, No. 47, September 1863, pp. 398-404.

Review of *Goblin Market and Other Poems*, in the *Athenaeum*, No. 1800, April 26, 1862, pp. 557-58.

Rossetti, Christina, "Goblin Market," in *The Complete Poems of Christina Rossetti*, edited by R.W. Crump, Louisiana State University Press, 1979, pp. 11-26.

Shalkhauser, Marian, "The Feminine Christ," in the *Victorian Newsletter*, No. 10, Autumn 1956, pp. 19-20.

Srimad Bhagavata Mahapurana, Part 1, translated by C.L. Goswami and M.A. Sastri, Gita Press, 1971, p. 20.

Swann, Thomas Burnett, "'Goblin Market':

Fantastic Masterpiece," in *Wonder and Whimsy: The Fantastic World of Christina Rossetti*, Marshall Jones Company, 1960, pp. 92-106.

Weathers, Winston, "Christina Rossetti: The Sisterhood of Self," in *Victorian Poetry*, No. 3, Spring 1965, pp. 81-9.

Further Reading

Bell, Mackenzie, *Christina Rossetti: A Biographical And Critical Study*, Kessinger, 2006.

> Bell's biography of Rossetti, first published in 1898, provides a fascinating insight into Rossetti and her family, the pre-Raphaelite circles in which they moved, and the literary life of the period.

Bowra, Cecil M., *The Romantic Imagination*, Harvard University Press, 1957.

> Bowra discusses the literary reputation of Christina Rossetti, ultimately defining her as a Romantic poet.

Bristow, Joseph, ed., *Victorian Women Poets: Emily Bronte, Elizabeth Barrett Browning, Christina Rossetti*, St. Martin's Press, 1995.

> This book contains a selection of essays by various critics on different poets, including one on Rossetti's religious poetry. The other essays are highly relevant to a study of Rossetti's work and the social and literary context in which she worked; the essays cover such topics as sexual power and politics, fallen women, and consumerism.

Marsh, Jan, *Christina Rossetti*, Viking, 1994.

> In this biography, Marsh makes use of letters and diaries to show how Rossetti's verse was a response to the people and events that shaped her life. Marsh quotes extensively from Rossetti's poetry and throws considerable light on her preoccupation with grief and death.

Rossetti, Christina, *Goblin Market*, illustrated by Arthur Rackham, Beaufort Books, 1985.

> This edition features illustrations by one of the greatest illustrators of children's literature, Arthur Rackham (1867-1939). As of 2007, it is out of print, but second-hand versions are available for purchase on the Internet.

Silver, Carole G., *Strange and Secret Peoples: Fairies and Victorian Consciousness*, Oxford University Press, 1999.

> Silver explores the widespread belief in, and fascination with, fairies in the Victorian period, further discussing the social anxieties that fueled this belief.

Lightning Source UK Ltd.
Milton Keynes UK
UKHW010633010419
340272UK00014B/832/P